P9-BYB-966

PENGUINS

New Lenox
Public Library District
120 Veterans Parkway
New Lenox, Illinois 60451

by JoAnn Early Macken

Reading consultant: Susan Nations, M.Ed., author/literacy coach/consultant

WEEKLY WR READER®
EARLY LEARNING LIBRARY

Please visit our web site at: www.earlyliteracy.cc
For a free color catalog describing Weekly Reader® Early Learning Library's
list of high-quality books, call 1-877-445-5824 (USA) or 1-800-387-3178 (Canada).
Weekly Reader® Early Learning Library's fax: (414) 336-0164.

Library of Congress Cataloging-in-Publication Data

Macken, JoAnn Early, 1953-
    Penguins / by JoAnn Early Macken.
       p. cm. — (Animals I see at the zoo)
    Summary: Photographs and simple text introduce the physical characteristics
and behavior of penguins, one of many animals kept in zoos.
    Includes bibliographical references and index.
    ISBN 0-8368-3273-6 (lib. bdg.)
    ISBN 0-8368-3286-8 (softcover)
    1. Penguins—Juvenile literature. 2. Zoo animals—Juvenile literature. [1. Penguins.
2. Zoo animals.] I. Title.
QL696.S473M32   2002
598.47—dc21
                                 2002016888

This edition first published in 2002 by
Weekly Reader® Early Learning Library
330 West Olive Street, Suite 100
Milwaukee, WI 53212 USA

Art direction: Tammy Gruenewald
Production: Susan Ashley
Photo research: Diane Laska-Swanke
Graphic design: Katherine A. Goedheer

Photo credits: Cover, title, pp. 5, 21 © James P. Rowan; p. 7 © Kent Foster/Visuals Unlimited;
p. 9 © Bill Kamin/Visuals Unlimited; pp. 11, 17, 19 © Greg W. Lasley/KAC Productions; p. 13
© Hugh Rose/Visuals Unlimited; p. 15 © Fritz Pölking/Visuals Unlimited

Printed in the United States of America

1 2 3 4 5 6 7 8 9 06 05 04 03 02

Note to Educators and Parents

Reading is such an exciting adventure for young children! They are beginning to integrate their oral language skills with written language. To encourage children along the path to early literacy, books must be colorful, engaging, and interesting; they should invite the young reader to explore both the print and the pictures.

Animals I See at the Zoo is a new series designed to help children read about twelve fascinating animals. In each book, young readers will learn interesting facts about the featured animal.

Each book is specially designed to support the young reader in the reading process. The familiar topics are appealing to young children and invite them to read — and re-read — again and again. The full-color photographs and enhanced text further support the student during the reading process.

In addition to serving as wonderful picture books in schools, libraries, homes, and other places where children learn to love reading, these books are specifically intended to be read within an instructional guided reading group. This small group setting allows beginning readers to work with a fluent adult model as they make meaning from the text. After children develop fluency with the text and content, the book can be read independently. Children and adults alike will find these books supportive, engaging, and fun!

— Susan Nations, M.Ed., author, literacy coach, and consultant in literacy development

I like to go to
the zoo. I see
penguins at
the zoo.

Penguins are strong, fast swimmers. They push through the water with their wings.

They steer with their feet and tails. Their smooth shapes help them glide in the water.

Penguins dive in the water for food. They eat shrimp, fish, and squid.

Penguins leap
out of the water
to breathe. They
leap out onto
the ice.

They stand in the sun to stay warm. They huddle in groups to stay warm.

Their feathers
keep them warm.
A layer of fat
keeps them
warm, too.

Penguins hop over the snow. They slide on their bellies like sleds. Whoosh!

I like to see penguins at the zoo. Do you?

Glossary

breathe — to take air into the lungs and let it out again

glide — to move smoothly and easily

steer — to direct the course of

For More Information

Books

Macken, JoAnn Early. *Polar Animals. Animal Worlds* (series). Milwaukee: Gareth Stevens, 2002.

Markle, Sandra. *Growing Up Wild: Penguins.* New York: Atheneum, 2002.

Tatham, Betty. *Penguin Chick.* New York: HarperCollins, 2002.

Web Sites

NATIONALGEOGRAPHIC.COM

www.nationalgeographic.com/kids/creature_feature/ 0101/penguins.html
For fun facts, video, audio, a map, and a postcard you can send to a friend

TerraQuest

www.terraquest.com/va/science/penguins/penguins.html
For photos and descriptions of penguins in Antarctica

Index

About the Author

JoAnn Early Macken is the author of a rhyming picture book, *Cats on Judy*, and *Animal Worlds*, a series of nonfiction picture books about animals and their habitats. Her poems have been published or accepted by *Ladybug*, *Spider*, *Highlights for Children*, and an anthology, *Stories from Where We Live: The Great Lakes*. A winner of the Barbara Juster Esbensen 2000 Poetry Teaching Award, she teaches poetry writing. She lives in Wisconsin with her husband and their two sons.